You Have
Called Me
by My Name

Other Books by Joseph A. Tetlow, SJ

Always Discerning: An Ignatian Spirituality for the New Millennium

Making Choices in Christ: The Foundations of Ignatian Spirituality

You Have Called Me by My Name

Praying with Father Joe Tetlow, SJ

LOYOLA PRESS.
A JESUIT MINISTRY
Chicago

LOYOLA PRESS.
A JESUIT MINISTRY

www.loyolapress.com

Cover art credit: Thomas Rochford SJ and JJ Mueller SJ/Jesuits USA Central and
Southern Province.

ISBN: 978-0-8294-5270-9
Library of Congress Control Number: 2021942229

Printed in the United States of America.
21 22 23 24 25 26 27 28 29 30 Versa 10 9 8 7 6 5 4 3 2 1

This book honors the memory of my father,
Joseph Allen Tetlow, Sr.

When He was very small,
you would caress Him with
your calloused hands
and cradle Him contentedly
against your workman's chest.
Now, Joseph, father to my brother Jesus,
I recall myself a little boy, and
ask you: let me stand against your side,
your arm around my slender shoulder
and my father (a Joseph, too)
on my other side, and me between,
because I need you now, and
Him, too, and
need's the only ground
I have to stand on as I call.
Will you, please, remembering Him—
stand by me—remembering—and
calling on you both? Amen.

Contents

Introduction

Jesuits in our many years of study were taught to think in Latin. I did it, and I conclude that some good might have come of it, but it's better to think in our own language. I think in English, with all its bluntness and vividness, approximations and misnaming. And English is the language God expects to hear from me—my English, the way I think and talk, the fire under liturgical ashes.

I mention this because so many seem to have been taught to pray as though prayer were a foreign language or an alien kind of mindfulness. Someone was taught to just "sit and let God talk to you," apparently expecting a "word."

That's odd, but it makes a valid point. God's language is silence, as the great theologian Karl Rahner taught. But God's silence is not being dumb—or deaf and dumb. God is not constrained, as we are, to use language. No. He comes in a vivid range of challenges and emotions, in a tornado of idea and desire, and within the pressures and solicitations of our surround.

When we pray in faith and hope, we take a time of silence to hear, feel, and reflect in Him, just the way a hawk soars on a wind when it goes into the sky, needing no instruction in how to fly.

The Church's magnificent tradition of a cloistered life of silence and prayer brings us contemplation. Most of us People of God, though, must pray in stolen silence, always urgent to cross the threshold into strident life. Our *lectio divina* must end in discernment as we beg for grace to know *Where just now, in all that's going on, am I to join my busy God creating and redeeming me and His cosmos?*

Sometimes—but very, very rarely, in my experience—the divine silence moves a man to a different space, changing a whole life, or altering an attitude or stance, or tearing out a fixed habit. God's language is silence—and the incarnation of His Truth.

We live believing that this Truth was once incarnate among us, living a life quite like our own. When I hear someone talk about their "image of God," I hope they learn that they are talking about their *image*, not about their *God*. We are given an image of God.

If we reach for it—this desire is the beginning of prayer—we turn to the One who said: *Learn of me, for I am meek and humble of heart.* As His difficult friend Saul of Tarsus put it for the Colossians: *He is the image of the unseen God, the firstborn of all creation.*

As we are reborn in Him, Jesus sends His Spirit. The Spirit comes from where Jesus is: in our flesh. She gives us outright the fierce decision that God lives and that God loves me and approves of me as I am—though much too well to leave me as I am.

For this God is at every instant powering evolution from within its tiniest elements to the furthermost masses in space. And powering the evolution within my own heart, so I do not need to "go into God's Presence." God is present in me already now: *Don't you understand that you are a temple of God, and God's Spirit dwells within you?*

Paul fumed at the Galatians—and at us when we forget. We are in God *now*; God is in us *now*. When we think we are praying but are not consoled in the present moment, we are thinking in a foreign language.

Back in our own language, the *image of the indivisible God* shows us what intimacy with God looks like. It's like intimacy with any other, the way Jesus did it. For some years, He spent whole days and weeks with men and women, the same men and women. He ate with them, walked, slept, talked with them—and talked and talked. And did some wonders, too, when someone needed one. He chose a dozen, and then grew very close to three: Peter, James, and John. But there was one everybody knew was His favorite. So it's that way with God.

He did what love in this kingdom of earth must do: cajoled, fed, corrected, fussed, blazed out, and loved to the end those He told in divine intimacy: *You are my friends.* This is intimacy with God in Christ, who tried to make us understand: *You are to love one another the way I have loved you.*

When Paul wrote that *He is the image of the unseen God,* he was reminding us that Jesus has given us a picture of exactly what intimacy with God looks like.

Every prayer is a momentary focus of eternal meaning.

So let us pray.

1.

Preparing What's to Come

Like the Sun, Lord, You Cherish Me

Like the sun, Lord, cherishing the earth,
warming it to life, lighting it to sight,
inciting little leaves to grow and burning off
       excess,
like the sun, Lord, You cherish me.
At every moment of my time
You warm me in my marrow,
You put sight into my eyes
and a steady rhythm in my blood.
If I can wonder for a while about your care,
the dark side of the earth feeling night,
I cannot fear for long.
Even fear, when I'm enclosed in it,
finds You inward there
and I am again content,
like the blue globe gently wheeling
in the sun
that would hurtle off to empty space
did the sun not cherish it most gently
but in might.
So ever cherish me, my Lord. Amen.

My Music Is Enough

You make Yourself, they tell me,
the music of the spheres, the heart
of heaven's harmonies.
Well, Lord,
I stand within this suite of glory
an old upright piano,
ivory off some keys, some wires broken,
twanging through the octaves.
Can I be called to play polyphonies
and fistfuls of climbing chords?
Should I join in cantatas and quartets?
    Well, God of harmonies, no. I cannot.
You know I cannot. But look,
I do not disdain the symphonies and songs,
I am not proud to crack the honeyed chords.
I just sit on my stool, head bowed to
the wonder of weightless harmonies
that I can't lift from my croaking keys.

So I sit content
in ragtime and in jazz,
my heart drumming to the blues for my
Holy God of heaven's harmonies.
May I hope, O Lord, oh, may I hope—
my prayer this syncopated stutter—
that ragtime is enough? Amen.

Quiet, All Alone

Now I come to quiet all alone,
no one else by me but You,
I have no special thoughts to think,
but marvel that I know You here,
Eternal Triune God—
in a little room, the middle of my heart—
here, where no one else can be,
just You and me for a little while.
    May I wonder, Lord—What is it like
to be One God, the only
One, unique and unimaginably alone?
Well, now I have a thought to offer You,
a little bit afraid to think it, even
in this middle room of quiet.
Here: I find myself unique—they tell me
that—unique and unrepeatable, too.
    Holy One, mighty One, now
I swiftly feel my littleness, am just
one other whom, magnanimous,
You make to share Your Oneness.
And now I feel a little shy with You,
alone.

Please, Lord, I beg:
Do share with me as well
Your boundless love
for all the other ones
You share our being with. Amen.

You Do Want My Love

Almighty and everlasting God,
as I am told, You hold me
in the palm of Your hand, and so I come to be.
But somewhat
puzzled, I confess,
how hard it is to feel You present
through the thrum of humdrum life.
And yet I yearn to cling to You—
cannot *not* yearn—whom I cannot
see or touch or tell into Your ear
that secret love hisses in me.
I yearn to cling to You in love
but cannot find the hold.

   Yet You are kind, Lord—
You let me live, a smeared and trembling
mirror of Your power at work
creating yet another man, shining
with light and joy but
shaking with the holy fear that
You do want my love—and always will.

Well, glory be to You, Father, I say,
and to You, His Son, in whom I do delight,
and to You, their joyous Spirit,
and I mean to make this holy shout forever,
and now for now. Amen.

In This Place I Know You

What if there were nothing here
when I come to be alone,
nothing but emptiness and dumb silence?
O most precious God,
how great You come to be against
blank nothingness, how dear to me,
the Most in all.
And in this place I know You
where I hang in nothingness,
for You are here and here I know You,
that You live, are great and beautiful
beyond all I see and feel, and know
that You love it all, are love,
and let me know, and ask me
—You *ask* me—to choose to love
You back—and let me rest in Your lap,
a bewildered child, and here
You let me stay for joy. Amen.

Send Your Spirit to Me

You free us, Lord, to grow
in wisdom and in grace
even as we grow in age,
as Jesus did.
I know that, good Father,
and yet I grow in age
clinging to what may not be
wisdom and is not grace,
aware that some of what is mine
You cannot like.
And yet, my Lord, I yearn for
what You like.
I beg You, send Your Spirit to me
and restore the sprouting holiness
of the infant child baptized.
Then I will remember whom
You love.
I beg this grace through Christ our Lord. Amen.

I Open My Heart

I open my heart to You,
Lord Jesus Christ.
Rummage around in me and
fling out what You do not like,
of thought and want,
of boldness and of fear.

Throw out all You do not like, all of it,
and teach my heart to not like it as well.
Then put instead, my Leader and my Lord,
put into my heart what You would like—
all that You would like.

I open my heart, like a young lover,
timid and brightened at what I do.
Then let me fall in love with You,
as I mean to do, and hope
to live in love with You—
will You put this hope in me?—
forever. Amen.

Embraced Forever

I didn't know I knew these things
until You came, encompassing all,
being All in it, if Other, loving,
"Love itself poured out," they say.
How dear, when I woke up so tense
at all I know and don't,
to find You, waiting for me
to wake, giving me to know that
You are here, always here, everywhere,
waiting—so beautiful and sweet You
embarrass language.
Your real makes my real an icon,
and You give me this knowing
that quells my dread of nothingness.
And I embrace You, to find You
have been embracing me forever
bringing me to know You
my Beloved.

2.

Who Dwell in Darkness and the Fear of Death

Such Insistent Gentle Love

Here at the root of Your mercy,
Holy One—You love me in my sin,
love me deeper, keeping on,
distrusting my repentance.
Were I not senseless I would fear,
feel waves of terror at
Your righteousness stern as lightning,
Your justice relentless as a sea
eating continents.
   Yet such is
Your insistent gentle love—that
You will not add Your grieving
to my burden when I sin,
bent down in guilt and shame. No.
Instead, You hold me in the silent
love at the root of Your mercy, patient
until my hurt makes me turn
and beg to get up again, again,
the way You want me. Then Your love
transmutes my grieving to a tenderness
like Your own, and I can love myself
into repentance—not indicted, but sweetly
impeached by Your mercy. Amen.

How Can You Love Me?

How can You love me, Lord Jesus,
holiness itself loving me a
patchwork of sin and selfishness,
so confounded by my doing and desiring
that I must fail to love myself.
You have loved me to death, Lord,
not the thing we say, "to death,"
but done in blood Your own,
done to earn the Father's right
to reconcile Your holiness to sin.
I am blind in my sins,
but that does not matter to You.
I live mindless of You,
but that does not matter to You, either.
For instead of hissing in anger,
You feel tender compassion for all
who suffer sin, perhaps because
You have suffered sin, too, suffered
more than any of us ever could know.
And You do not let that matter, either.
You just love me still—and for all that,
You are the Holy One, still. Can You
make me more like You, please? Amen.

A Little Ping of Pure Intent

How can You love me, Lord Jesus,
repentance, not regret, most holy Lord,
I wish my heart were strong enough to hold.
For if the guilt that I invite by deeds
pales pink before the scarlet sins of giants,
the stains in my little soul
are every hue as deep as theirs
in unloving selfishness.

　　How can my heart, this little drum,
manage the muted symphony of sorrow
that ought to sound from every whispered sin?
Maybe, Lord of harmonies,
I can ding my whole self
like love told out from a chime,
a little ping of pure intent
suspended on a string of yearning.
Could that sound to Your merciful ear,
most holy Lord,
enough like repentance?

Now I Am in Need

You healed the sick and lame,
Lord Jesus Christ,
and gave sight to the blind and
sound to the deaf and dumb.
You touched to clean wholeness many lepers
and raised the untimely dead to live again.
You refused to condemn the adulterous woman,
and gently took a murderous thief with You
to heaven, because he asked.
And after Peter Your impulsive friend
denied You, You joined him in his wretchedness
and bound him again in Your love.

    Well, Lord Jesus, now I am in need.
Please hear my prayer.
Forgive me my guilt and my sins.
Teach me to bear the burdens sin lays on us
as You once bore them just for love of us.
Teach me to love as You have loved
and to rejoice in our Father's mercy
as steady as the tides
and glad as sunrise. Amen.

I Repent Again

God our Father, I have sinned.
Long after I had set myself against it,
I sinned again, and now I hurt.
And still I know that I can sin, again,
and will till I am dead,
but just for now, I hurt.
I groan again that I am sorry again
and repent again—and I confess:
I am afraid.

  I beg you, Father, not to let this sin
follow on to other sins, one sliding to another.
Stop it now, impatient for once, mighty God,
with me who am not worth Your work
and deserve nothing better than to sin.
Stop me now, most merciful and just,
because You can and I cannot. You can,
You can hold me back from doing yet again
what once I firmly set myself not to do.
Hold on to me, I have no right to ask
but do—hold on to me—I beg You,
hold on to me
because I keep falling. Amen.

Love Wrapped in Fear

I am afraid of dying,
great Lord of Life,
I have to tell You,
a terror in my gut about that dark—
not dark enabling sleep,
great Lord of Light,
but dark from which
I will not once come back
to what I know of life and light.
I will be gone.

So I am told to hope, told
that I must hope in what
You said, all *rising from the dead*,
and trust in what they said
You did: Rose. Came back.

But how, I wonder—how
did You come back? What like?
I still sit in the dark that I know.
I tell You, Lord of Truth,
ashamed, I feel this fear.

Then do You mind
how my trust in You comes
wrapped in fear?

Be not afraid, You said,
so I think You knew their love
for You came wrapped in fear.
What I think will not offend You,
I think? Or better yet, I beg. Amen.

Call Me to an Agile Love

What a terror tore your soul,
Simon Peter, fisherman from Galilee,
when you heard yourself say—
now, now, and a third time—
I do not know him,
into whose eyes you suddenly stared,
who, saying nothing, only looked.

O my friend, once weak in holiness,
instruct my heart to let my wrongness go,
to kneel in the ashes of my honor,
to press my forehead
into the flesh of His forgiveness.

O Peter, paradigm of holy weakness,
call me to the agile love
you called the paralytic to in Lydda—
Get up! Take up your cot!—
and call me back to life as simply
as you said to Dorcas—
Talitha! Wake up!—
Brash as you back then, I ask:
Wake me,
wake me up,
wake me up to Him. Amen.

Wanting More and More to Love

I have no claim on You,
who justly claim as Yours
all that is, has been, and
is as yet to be.
My only standing is Your love,
in which You think of me
and out of which You fashion me.
Marred as I have made myself,
I come
not bringing to You what I've done,
but begging You for Your own love,
to let me be a little longer
sinning and grieving still
but wanting
more and more to love
You, to love You for Your love
and not for mine.
Just for Your love. Amen.

Turning Away from Sin

Now I have turned away
from that sin I longed
to live without
but could not quit,
loving and merciful God,
I know it is Your gift
that it is gone.
I clung to it before, inanely sure
it was me and what I had to do,
and still I feel the strain—
I might reach back.

   Praise You, Lord, who pierced
the armor of my sloth,
and gave me to quit.

   Pierce me, fierce One,
for I will not hold Your love
blended in my obdurate brain,
until I fold Your love and mercy
in my heart. Amen.

3.

Blinking in Broad Daylight

What Do I Bring to You?

How You chose me from the multitudes
to fight beside You as You make a kingdom,
Lord Jesus, and make me Your man,
confounds me. Even crying *Yes!*
I wonder what I bring to You
who brought Yourself to me.
Yet here I am—so incomplete a man
beyond imperfect to hurting,
so full of yearning to be more
but empty of the grace to grow there.
Then, Lord, what sins will mar my time—
You know they are always the same,
and so the shame will be—the same.
But I cannot fret at that. I will not,
starting to be Yours who loves me
amazingly beyond the multitudes.
Boldly, then I say:
　　To my Lord, I give
　　the hours of my life and
　　the use of my death.
That little I do give
and You will make, enough. Amen.

Remembering the Shepherds

O Christ! Your birth begins
a journey foreordained for the little time
allotted each of us. And every minute
You later spent gave Your heart
a sadder grasp of how we waste our
days and years. Look, Lord Jesus,
look into my feckless time
and empty heart.
Remember shepherds leaving
flocks of woolly wariness
to spend a giggling hour watching You,
a little fellow in His mother's arms.

  O Jesus, let me leave aside
a flock of bleating self-blame
to watch You for a sunny while
showing what to do instead
of busily wasting the little time
that's given each of us—
at least this sunny while watching
You at Your mother's breast
and in Your father's arms,
resting joyfully in love. Amen.

He Has Come into My Shrinking Soul

I am not a one, Holy God,
can claim to pray with sinless lips.
My mouth is full of trash, a perfect logjam
of factoids and of splintered truth.
Yet in this wreck—somehow in this wreck—
Your Truth joins things together
and I know *that my Redeemer lives* and
He has come into my shrinking soul and
brought with Him the Holy Spirit
and all good things besides.
So here in my heart You dwell,
as in a shabby crib quite like the one
the Son was born in.
I'll be like the shepherds, then,
hearing *Glory to God in the highest*,
glistening with wonder and joy
standing in their stinky fieldhand clothes.
You never minded them then.
I beg you will not now
mind me, either, as I say my *Glory!* Amen.

Wisdom, Age, and Grace

The way You took to grow, Lord Jesus—
wisdom, age, and grace—
from a little pup to the greatest friend of all,
You started at a mother's breast, the Lady Mary's,
and in strong Joseph's fathering arms.
You wandered through the kitchens and
      the yards
of family friends and played young games.
Along the ordinary ways of fun and hurt,
You became: Yourself—The Way to be the
      greatest friend.
Well, just now, Lord, we won't attend to woe.
For this little while, we imagine a tranquil infant
buckled in breech-clout and wrapped in blanket,
held against the woman's bosom and the
      man's chest,
and this memory makes us glad for a while
to go along Your Way, *wisdom, age, and grace*,
hoping what You hoped,
to live among friends,
and then to make You ours
and to be Yours. Amen.

I Trust That You Can Manage Me

While I am wrestling still,
Lord Jesus Christ,
with what I call "my ways,"
You come to me as King
and place me in Your ranks.
You make me soldier, fighting
enemies hardly separate from my self.
You make me diplomat, balancing
my own desires
that then escape, unbalanced.
I am to stand under Your banner?
Lord, have You no one else,
no one who could with ease
do what I can barely manage?
I tell You simple truth, Lord.
Is Your love blinding You
to who I really am? No. It's not—and
when I stumble and falter and fall,
well—You already knew.
    This much I can do honestly:
trust that You can manage me
in all my "ways"—and out of them.
Lord Jesus, I beg that be enough. Amen.

Thinking of Peter

You liked him, Lord, Your Peter,
dense and impulsive as he was.
You liked him; he was Your man.

   The others knew it, too, and
maybe James and John,
asking for places at Your elbows,
enacted jealousy the others felt.

   Your man would not have noticed.
Peter could not imagine any reason
for being with You than Yourself,
just You, Yourself.
He would then push his way into
an unjust yard where You were pelted
and declared unclean,
a dinghy lunging into surf, crashing on stones,
no matter what, to share his Lord's peril
as the tide rose to swallow You.
You loved him for that—for all of that.

   He was Your man, and makes me think
that I might be, too, dense as ever he was
and maybe more impulsive yet
to put myself always in Your ranks.

He makes me hope You might want me,
still, what's left of me from sin.
Because the truth is, if You ask,
I will answer like Peter,
You know I love You.
Three times—and truer every time,
and *please know that I love You.* Amen.

What Is This Hole in Me?

What is it makes me want You,
Lord of everything that is,
whom I have never seen and cannot touch,
so much that nothing else will do?
What is this hole in me
that You fit like a star its pointy place,
and any other thing put there,
leaves it empty anyhow?
   You hold now many whom I love,
Lord Jesus Christ, whom I grieve
gone on without me—but they
didn't leave this hole. It's Yours.
I don't know how, unless this thing
about You loving me is real,
and every longing I might have
for someone else is hazy hankering,
a wishy yen compared to this black hole,
its cosmic wind pulling me into its heart.
   Well, Lord greater than the cosmos,
Come into this hole in me—
and then if you will let me

I'll find some way along with You
to make the hole my own place, too.
If that's all right, Lord Jesus?
Is that what we will do? Amen.

Lady Mary, Teach Me to Love

Though I have loved another,
and another and another—
You are my Lady, the only
one now can ever be, my Lady.
And you have let this be because
you know me not in part,
but as Your Son shows me
to you, His Lady Mother, whole,
fragile, bold, and antic—but
His friend.
So all that shames me in my self,
what false and sour notes
make my love a wildly cacophonic
song of joy, you're deaf to, like Him,
because you know my inward self
the way He knows it—the way
He chose to make it—radiant
with the love that is His love
in me, His, whom you taught to love.

Lady Mary, teach me to love
as you taught Jesus to love,
for I would be your fated son
as He was once, your little Son
who is now the Lord of all
though you are still His Lady Mother
as I beg you will be, Lady Mary,
mine. Amen.

What Thomas Said

What sort of man would say,
"We'll go with Him," who planned
to walk through land mines of the powers'
deadly purposes and plots to kill—walk
to bring dead Lazarus back
from where
this trip could well send them all?
You said it, Thomas, right out,
no doubt: *Go and die with Him.*
Well, you teetered, Thomas—your voice
once quick and strong *Save us, we perish*—
you teetered when stone gritted over dark
and Him within it—the closing, final.

And after that, you would not believe.
You wanted Him so hard, your
wanting had to hide behind a shield of doubt.
He knew. He knew you were afraid—He's gone,
your wanting Him an anguish. So, tenderly,
He put your hand into His wounds—
and then you knew your loyal
love flaming under all the ashes.

Thomas, sir, will you ask Him, please,
to put my hand to His heart?
Because loyal I may be like you, but
there are times I teeter, too. Amen.

Love and Blunder Both

Well, that
this is what I had been doing all along,
I did not know, Jesus my Lord,
until I heard You say,
as though in thanks,
You are the men who stood by me
in my trials, while I had thought
all along I barely managed
snatching loyal love from blunder.
Then to find in the end
that You had tallied all along
the love and blunder both,
and reached through them to me,
then chose to keep me still Your man—
to find this in the end
is to wake to blazing sun
lighting somehow where all along
I stood, and dawning on a dullard,
oh, but willing, willing,
that I am one You call Your friend. Amen.

Woman with a Broken Heart

She had a broken heart, the woman
who washed Your feet with her tears
and dried them with her hair.
She had a broken heart, Lord Jesus—
as anyone with sense could see.
But the uptight people You were dining with
did not bother with sense.
They tasted her vile reputation.
That's what they smelled. In righteousness,
that's what they saw, not her.

   That's not what You saw, merciful Lord.
You saw a woman who wanted love
and had looked in all the wrong places.

   O Lord, we count on what You see,
with Your gentle gaze of mercy.
For You see me—You see all of us—
seeking love where it is not and not giving it
where we could. Give us a broken heart,
like hers,
You who come seeking sinners,
who are the Christ,
and seeking us, too. Amen.

Waiting

Listen to me, Lady Mary,
mother of Jesus of Nazareth
spouse of Joseph, David's son.
Listen to me, please, good mother,
complain:
I have to wait for Him. And wait.

   I know you had to wait, yourself,
once your word was *yes!*
You had to wait while you swole
so slowly, and your virgin breasts.
But all those months, Lady Mother,
your spirit could rejoice in God your Savior
as your whole self grew great
without the slightest hurt of doing wrong.

   Not me, Lady, not me.
I have to wait while I become what
God my Maker wants: a rock worn down
by streams of gritty fault and sin. And
it would help now were I consoled,
mulled in a flowing wine of grace.

    Well, Mother,
would you ask your Son,
please, Lady, as you did before,
to maybe do in me
what at Cana feast He did before:
change drums of watery waiting
into the choicest wine of patience
to mull my waiting?
That will make me very glad, Lady. Amen.

How Can I Know You?

How can I know you, Lord Jesus Christ?
You lived so long ago, in a far place
now covered with concrete and The People—
there again but not theirs again.
It is not really where you walked,
not anymore, but really seemed so
when I went—I surely wanted it to be.
To know You, Lord, I read the stories
we remember and I guess they tell me
who You are. At least they make
my thinking bright and my heart's breath
catch. I guess that's how I know You,
which I yearn for keenly and You said
You wanted: *Learn of me*, You said.

   But how? So sharply
do I yearn to love You,
I have to hope my way of doing it's not wrong.
I wish I could touch your shoulder—
No, I wish You'd put Your arm around
my shoulder and take my head in Your hands,
and shake it a little like I think You did Peter's.

There's a third thing, Lord, if You'll let me.
The fullest truth is, I want an abrazo for us,
the way good friends do in my land.
Is it so very wrong to wish for that, though
You are so great and God and all?
I think I am afraid to ask and
still I want it, Jesus, my Lord, because
You did, You *called us friends*. Amen.

I'll Go with You

I'll go with You, Lord Jesus Christ,
I'll go with You into whatever waste
Your Spirit leads.
I'll go with You where You will go
among the hurting and the lost.
I'll go with You, borrowing
courage I do not have.
It will not matter, if I go with You,
that my own heart will fail,
half an enemy deep within—
but not as deep within
as You already there,
leading me where
I had never thought to go
and where I would not on my own.
But now I will, wherever,
I'll go with You, Your Spirit
making sure I hear when
You call. Please? Amen.

What Do You Want?

They brought You,
Lord, a man born seeing
but now gone blind. He groveled
before You, fearful whether
You might heal him as You
healed so many more.
You raised him to his knees
and asked: *What do you want me
to do for you?* He went blind
and lost his world and wanted it
back. Simply, he said.
You took his face into Your hands,
and with Your thumbs, wiped blindness
from his eyes and he blinked open
to see—to see You smiling
into his face.

   O Christ, in my heart I grovel
before You, as much as I am worthy to.
You take my face into Your hands,
and ask me, *What do you want?*,
and I will gasp, terrified at what to hope—
that I may see to love You
as Bartimaeus surely did. Amen.

If Only I Could Hear You Say My Name

How strange that I should love this way,
that just to say Your name, *Jesus,*
or even hear the sound of it, *Jesus, Jesus,*
makes me content—or mostly so,
until I think to yearn for something else.
It's this:
What if I could hear *You* say *my* name?
O Lord, if ever I could hear You say my name.
I would never need another thing, ever,
to keep faithful to Jesus in heart and deed,
to fling myself into Your work, Jesus,
or else to wait, still in the dark, for what
        You want.
If only I could hear You say my name.
   Next best: I will imagine it, Lord,
when next I take the Host,
sure that You are come entire.
Your voice will be resounding in the Bread,
its tone and timber more than hinted in
        the Wine.

That will have to be enough for now,
for I think, my Lord, that this is how
You wanted us to hear You say our
                names. Amen.

Holy Potter, Finish This Work

I begin this time of prayer,
Spirit of the living God,
hoping yet again with all my heart
to find what You would do in me.
I think at times I have been tried by fire,
and am a finished vessel, waiting
only to be filled up with Your will.

    The truth would be: my times of fire
are more the holy Potter, wroth
at my misshaping sins,
mashing down my clay in desolation,
meaning to start again. Yet
even crushed, I hope and mean to take
the shape You want in me, and I feel You,
Holy Potter, finishing the work,
molding me like Him in whose image
I am being made but fear to take.

O Spirit of the Living God, I say,
shape me as You shaped the Son,
even if You do as I am terrified
to think You might.
Only bring me when *it is finished*
to Yourself, finally made
the man You are hoping for
in eternity. Amen.

Thinking of Joseph

Joseph of Nazareth, David's son,
You went off sometimes to walk at night
and let the cool soothe the bubbling in
     your veins
and the quiet smooth the knots in muscles
and the dark hide your chagrin.
You were loyal fully, Joseph, and entirely good.
Though you were mighty in fighting urges
and the need men have to feel our strength
and to finish out what must be done,
you waited and waited, and walked in the dark.
You loved her, the young and lovely lady
     given you
by God to keep, along with a heartset how
     to love.
And you did, you kept them both.
You kept the lady until the time was safe for her.
You loved the Son who was your own and not
     your own.
You took Him in your lap when He was little
and to your side, a limber boy,
holding His hands on your tools and
His mind on your Father.

Then you let Him go and
got no glory for your greatest work.
Walk with me, safe and mighty man,
all the times I need to walk in the cool of the
        night. Amen.

4.

In the Crimson of the Setting Sun

Say the Truth One More Time

You stood, Lord Jesus, head bowed,
looking at the ground
while they lied and hedged through
thickets of false charges and fake crimes.
Then You spoke the truth one more time and
they tore their garments, pulled their hair,
and yelled their throats raw cursing You.

   Lord Jesus, say the truth one more time
and brand it in my heart:
You are the Christ.
You suffered for my sins.
I would break my heart with sorrow
over this—but
do not know how.
You knew. You broke Your heart
in sorrow that they would not see.

   I stand with You, Lord, my head bowed,
yearning to know Your heart
and sorrow with You.
Share Your passion with me, Lord?
I am afraid to ask—
and do. Amen.

Now, an Eternity of Dark

In the crimson of a setting sun
the *Dawn from on High*—sank—
into the dark where those who hated Him
wanted Him to go. O Christ Jesus!
Now they have done the doing and
now they know who did it: not
them but You—the One they knew
to hate but not to fear.

   Now they know—that fear
they would not feel when facing Him
now crushes them with Him gone.
From His tomb—that memory,
His word about the rising of the Son.
The third day will come,
but now, an eternity of dark,
of waiting in terror, of ancient liturgies
with slaughtered bloody lambs
and dry hosts and a cup of wine.

   O Christ, I want You in this dark—not
earth's, not theirs—my dark—a dark
of doubt livelier than faith—as
day by day I watch for You
in the crimson of the setting sun.

Do not elude me, dying Lord,
I beg You—do not, bloodied Savior,
sink away from me into the hateful dark. Amen.

Son of Holy Silence

Where my mourning meets
my emptiness,
Son of holy silence, there
I find You sweating in terror
of what You know must come.
I stretch beside You, sweating too,
in terror of an emptiness I feel
but cannot name except to say
I fear myself in what must come.

   And so I cling and clutch at You,
who somehow brought Your holy silence
into the clangor of a human self
and filled our emptiness
with love not so apparent now.
For now You sweat in silence
having told the Father how it hurts.

   What can I dare to hope for here—
except that You will not,
ever, leave me dead silent.
O Christ, even in Your agony,
find breath to say my name—
please let me hear You say my name. Amen.

If You Help Me, I Will Die in Hope

You hang in agony, my Lord Jesus,
naked and disdained, in pain so fierce
it almost doesn't matter that Your mother's there.
But You already know that You will rise.
You told Your friends: You will live again.
As Your blood leaks from Your body,
You will not let hope leak from Your soul.
Then Your life leaves, a howl from Your guts
and one last sobbing breath: *Into Your hands*
I commit my spirit.

   You die, faithful Lord, in hope
that strings Your pains, a golden thread
unbroken by infidelity.
My Lord Jesus, my life is no golden thread
but a ribbon snarled with knots.
Still, if You help me, I will die in hope.
I promise I will die in hope, die
as You did at least this far, that
I will die the way our Father has decreed.
And I beg my leaving breath will be
Into Your hands I commit my spirit,
like You in this, if, all along, pathetically
in so little else. Amen.

May I Hope That It's Enough?

What did Peter feel, Lord Jesus Christ,
when he saw in every eye he looked into
a blurred reflection of his triple sin,
his fevered claim he knew You not—
surrounding him a fence of mirrors showing
him failing, failing, failing and a failure—
what did Peter feel?
Some would say, gently, not loud,
but in the angle of their glances,

   "We know, Peter, Rock, we all know."
But who of us can claim, come a test,
we would not do as you have done?
They knew that they had done
as you did, Peter, Rock,
the ones who ran—they knew.

   Is this why You let them do it, Lord?
why You let Peter stream his impulse
and everyone blame him with their eyes?

Why You let Judas do what Judas did—
the Judas whom You loved—
so You could see in our eyes a puzzlement,
at least a puzzlement, if not a half-felt fear,
that You let them do it—and then
might let us do it, too?

   We cannot say we understand, Lord Jesus,
but when I have betrayed myself and
look to You I find the pain in Your eyes
somehow not damning but sharing—
the pain of failing layered in upon
the pain of being failed. For
You failed, too.
When I fail and then I turn to You and
say I love You, I see You see
I love You anyhow, like Peter,
and I love You, like all of them.
May I hope, Lord, as they must have,
that it's enough? Amen.

We Stumble and Fall

We stumble and fall, Lord Jesus,
and on the ground we find You there before us,
three times fallen, weak and helpless.
But You get up time and time again, and
finish what You must do.
When searing sin drove You from our flesh,
the Father plunked You back into our flesh,
again among Your stumbling people.

   And You came, wounds and all,
so filled with exaltation that You talked
and talked, walked and talked
all the way to Emmaus and then for forty days,
putting off going home to the Father
just to stay with friends.

   We know, Lord—You walk with us still,
yearning for us to come to You and
be healed with the Bread and the Cup.
Then, when we fall again and
find You there again, we rise again
and can go on until the Father
gives us Your victory and we, too, go home.

Until then, most merciful Redeemer,
we stumble and fall, but
this is mercy—
You are always there. Amen.

I Cling to You with Slipping Hands

Here in the Passion comes a time,
Lord Jesus of Nazareth, a time
of mortal flesh excoriated by our sins.
Now I seem to bleed, at every pore,
the anguish of futility.
There come no hands, no pills,
to dull my sweating grief
and I see no other way, but it is wrong.
I feel no lack of breath, but
can emit no single sound to console.
And hope has gone the way of sweat.
   Ah, Christ! You know from that time
in the garden, You know how anguish
exudes the last reserves of self and
You begged the Father, "Do it differently"—
and the Father answered nothing.
   Oh, Christ, help! I cling to You
with slipping hands.
Then do You cling to me! Please,
You cling to me! Amen.

I Haven't Cared Till Now

Because my Friend has died,
I break out weeping,
astonished that I cry at all for You,
my Lord crucified.
I wonder whether my hot tears are Peter's
when he gagged at what he'd done—
our souls pierced with sorrows the flesh feels
just remembering the cross.
I cannot grieve like him. I have not done
what Peter did. I never did deny You, Lord,
but I did worse: I haven't cared.
O Christ, I haven't cared.
I haven't cared at all,
till now. And now I weep
—not for not caring, but—
as though I never knew,
because my Friend has died.
I wonder, Lord. Maybe our weeping now
means You no longer need to weep.
I do not know. I cannot care
because my Friend has died. Amen.

5.

So This Is
What It Means

Jesus' Wounds and Ours

You bear in Your own body mortal wounds,
Lord Jesus Christ,
which, were You not immortal now,
would wound You once again to death.
O Lord, I carry in my flesh some wounds
that pierce through marrow to my soul,
and I am mortal still,
whom wounds will do to death.
   Lord Jesus Christ, as You won the Doubter
by wearing wounds, do me a tender kindness
by holding back with wounded hand
my hands from wounding my soul
or hurting those You gave me.
Do this, my Lord, for all of us,
for if You'll never sink to death again,
we can and will, whom You embraced in love,
and need You showing us Your wounded self
so we can know how we will rise.
Do this, my Lord, for all of us. Amen.

How to Believe Now

The Dawn from on High Will Break Upon Us
was the promise made
through holy prophets, long ago dead.
Now, Lord of Light and Life,
we marvel at our grasp of firm faith
and wonder how we can believe
what we believe as rightly
as sun rise and wedded passion.
You're in our flesh again and still,
though now You feel much further
in the past and all we have of flesh
is one another, muddling and believing,
and I for one would more than likely
be agnostic or at least not caring
except for my friend Lee who believes
and my best cousin Mary and Paul Schott
and my niece who prays though she's
a lawyer and runs a university.
    Oh. Lord! Oh—
Is this what You had in mind?
Our resurrection out from doubt
to loving one another as You loved?
Well, Lord, yes! Think of that!

The Dawn from on High already
broke upon us and we weren't watching.
Well, Alleluia! I say. And
let's just make this plenty enough
for now. Alleluia and amen!

To Mary of Magdala

In the empty garden
where no one waited anymore,
the other women running back
to tell about the empty tomb,
you would not leave
because His corpse was gone,
Mary of Magdala, and then
you asked the workman where it was
and please to tell you so you could
tend Him better than that other day
but you really wanted at least
to touch Him one last time.
And then the Workman said
Mary
and you did what I wish I could
with all my heart, and He would
gently say, with my name, *Don't*
cling to me, and I would suddenly
know what I was doing,
what I did not know until I did it,
what I have wanted forever.

If I pray your name, Mary,
His loving, close-held friend,
will you please remind Him of
this? Amen.

I Must Wait, Wrapped in Hope

What worlds must wait for us
the other side of darkness,
You have kept a secret from us,
Lord Jesus, drawing us to hope and
breathing fire into the ashes of our days.
I must wait for a splendor yet to come
that will make our crimson sunrise pale
and the lucid blue of oceans murk.
So I must wait, Lord Jesus, wrapped in hope.
This helps, to know that You had hope, that
You waited once inside the dark—the rest of
a day, a night, another day, another night—
You waited till the Father wanted, and then
You rose, Yourself,
the radiant promise of our flesh.
I guess it has to be enough for hope
that You did that, You waited.
I do not find it really hard, Lord Jesus,
waiting in the darkness and
the shadow of death, when I recall it's
not for heavens splendid beyond dreaming
that we wait—that I wait. It's for
You. Amen.

Given Your Spirit, We Call You

No one knows the secret place
where we meet, beloved Lord.
Even when we pray out loud,
still no one knows the secret place.
   This must be infinity, how
You reach everywhere like sunlight
yet hide like the eyeless dark so
that each of us knows
and none of us knows
Who You are but You. Yet
given Your Spirit, we call You.
   Urged by angels—
lassoed in Your love, and
led alone into this secret place,
I am come once more, Beloved,
and I find
You yet again already here. Amen.

Please, Lord, Want Us Back

Did You wake one of the guards,
Lord Jesus, when You rose—
or beckon one already up—
to see a man made alive again and
clean—flesh smooth and whole—
a radiant joy lighting a corpse no longer dead?
    Far from dead—forever far from dead—
Your winding sheets gathered in a heap,
a linen jumble stained with blood and serum
in blotched patterns shocking even Death,
and stunning it aware of a dread:
These marks wrote the end of my dominion.
    And You, risen Lord Jesus,
ready now to bring back from defeat
the ones who ran and the one who denied,
knowing that You know he really meant
to love You closer and tried it on his own—
and the others knowing You had sent them off
for safety and now wanted them back.

Lord Jesus, when we try to love You closer
and end up falling yet again to some fake surety,
Peter-like, please want us back—
and Thomas, too—please
want us back,
always, always want us back. Amen.

6.

And Then Afterwards

Alone but Not Alone

When I come alone seeking You,
silent Lord Jesus,
I cannot hear Your voice as Peter did:
Courage, it's me, and so I stay alone.
You went alone a lot, Lord—You
spent the nights in prayer.
But not alone, You said,
the Father with You.
Always.
What ways will lead me there,
Lord Jesus, where I am not alone?
Lead me those ways there,
where alone is where You are.
And the Father.
And the Spirit, too.
Jesus, silent Lord, take and keep me
there. Amen.

A Friend Missed

You were such a friend, Jesus, Mary's son,
so deep in Your love that men and women both
followed You around, doing nothing,
just being with You in Your mobile shop.
So I share in each Communion how You know
that now, in just this time, I miss my friends.
They are jobbers in Your mobile shop, but
scattered now because You told us all to go.
I miss those men who share my sandy soul,
those women who caress like desert air—
You knew them, Lord, in Your time here—
those few, so few that once we scatter
we are green tufts of grass in drought. But
their love in me is yeasty life in sweet-roll dough,
swelling my chest, blocking my windpipe,
dimming my eyes with happy water
even while I grieve the missing presence
and the warmth. You know, sweet Friend,
You know what I mean.

For this I also know—
so many don't and how do they endure?—
You share the nailing pain of absence so entirely
that You contrived a way to stay among
Your hosts of friends as if not gone.
Stay close, Lord Jesus, who chose to call us
          servants,
friends,
for I am lonesome now, missing mine. Amen.

Since I Am Clay

Since I am clay, Lord of Light,
  Since I am clay, I bring in my hands
all the springs and deserts,
all the seas and mountains,
to praise Your holy Name.
  Since I am clay, I raise my eyes
and hold my hands palm-up
to cup the little praise I give Your holy Name.
  Since I am clay, I take the Bread of Life
and sip the Cup of Blessing,
my heart purring quiet joy
my body tingling live thanks
and spirit dancing joy—
  since I am clay and
yet I know and speak
Your holy Name. Amen.

I Would Walk Unanxious

You risked in ways I know, though even more,
Lord Jesus, Son, equal to the Father.
You clung to Peter though You read him plain,
his strengths and faults, sure to lead
to his denial, and yet You held him,
and washed the feet of Judas as he ate
sharing the bread You shared Your Self.
You knew the end he beckoned to
and calmly walked with him.
How could You do this—unless
You knew in Your heart the Father
always acting, always caring, always guiding.
You knew Him making life in You,
no matter what.

   O Lord, if I could trust as You trust
and be content that God does and can and cares,
I would walk unanxious, fearing nothing else
but Him, the One You loved and trusted.
Could You help me, Jesus, know Him,
as You know Him—Father
—in all my being and doing? Amen.

Now I Go to Rest

Now I go to rest, my Lord Jesus,
though inward and outward both
I leave a lot undone.
I feel the noise of worry
clanging in my spirit
that I leave a lot to You. But
I ask You, Lord, what else am I to do?
   And then I wonder that
You never seem to mind when
I turn to You, finally, when
there's no one else and nowhere
else to go. I know You are the Way
and, now I call to mind,
the Destination.
   So when every day is done,
and all I care about is put away,
I want to say to You—
marveling it should matter to You—
that for me,
You are besides whom
there is nothing else.

I know that's true and makes
one thing I cannot leave undone:
So here's my heart.
And now I go to rest. Amen.

Together We Weep

Like You before Your Lazarus interred,
I stand and weep, confronted by a void
where loving souls had been.
Now Donald gone, like Pat and Vince before.
Now I am as Martha was, made bold
to ask almost accusingly—
Where was Your friendship
when love needed You to help?
I would resign the faith
and wander all alone in wastes—
did we not remember
how a flaw in timing
kept You from Your standard deed
of healing out of love,
and Lazarus died,
and let You share with us
the loss.
And so You wept, You even groaned
along with all creation.
Then You called forth life, risen.

I know that I will come to that,
I know—so will we all.
But now, until it comes,
I stand with You and
You with me, and together
we weep. Amen.

Unready but Anointed

How you came to be a saint, King David,
gives me consolation and a way ahead.
You were chosen and anointed,
underage, ready for nothing
but tending sheep and slinging stones at wolves.
God knew what He wanted, though; you
          were good.
You knew how to fight wars and win hearts.
You knew how to manage and how to lead.
You knew, saint David, you also knew
how to sin.
   Your many wives were not enough for you.
Loaded with yourself, you took one not
          your own.
You grabbed for little gods when success called
and you consulted the underworld in a mist
of sulfured insolence before the God of gods.
   And for all that, God the almighty and all
          merciful
chose you and anointed you
and refused to give His passionate love defeat.

He made you a saint, King David, His man,
and I choose you for my saint, who understands
how we are underage and ready for nothing
when it comes to holy. You understand—
how well you understand.
Remember me before Him, then,
who chose me, too, underaged, unready,
but anointed as His own. Amen.

Give Me Today What to Do Today

From among the richest of the gifts You
give me, Lord, I mean to offer You in thanks
this morning the best that comes to hand.
   Lord mighty God, You assign
to their places
huge galaxies and to moons an orbit, yet
move the wings of every little chickadee.
You bring the sun around in the morning
and guide the night hawks in their flight.
And yet with all that, Fathering God,
You tend to each of us
as though You had no more to do. Then
shape in me, caring Lord, my return to You.
I would like to live as Your Son Jesus lived,
who did every day only what He saw
You doing, and could say in the end,
I have done the work You gave me to do.
This will be the richest gift that I can give, and
this is how I want to live, mighty Lord,
this day and every other day to come.

You know, Lord of galaxies and little birds,
that I cannot unless You show me how,
and give me today what to do today,
and every day the same, in Jesus' Name.
Like Him then, may I come to say,
I have done the work You gave me to do. Amen.

I Would Not Be a Fake

I have learned to do the things
men do who love You—at least, as I am told.
I do them, Lord Jesus, mostly, if not so very well.
In my heart I wonder what days mean
when I feel false though I keep doing
with my hands and halfway with my heart
what a man is meant to do,
one called to walk with You as with a Friend.

I would not be a fake, Jesus of Nazareth.
You walked with one at least who was,
who had better not been born.
I fear his fate as I keep groping for my way.

O Lord, You know my heart—face me with
what makes a man's love real, that
You know I can, with help, endure.
Walk with me through trials I fear because
they strip the false and then leave—what,
I do not know. I look to You,
Lord, who loves me wisely,
to fill up the half-truths I trust and to scour
from my heart the false attached there.

Make me Your lithe and steely lover,
if that is what You want.
I think I know that that is what I want.
I think. Please? Amen.

From No to Yes

I know You mean to heal me
when You come, Lord Jesus,
like the man who yelled and yelled
until You took his face into Your hands
and he said, *yes, yes,* until You
wiped away his blindness
with Your thumbs.
I know You mean to give me sight
where I was blind before
and I'll say *yes* when You touch me.
But when, Lord, when? You know
how blind I have long been,
and have said *no*
so long that I do not know now
what else to say but *no*
in the little corners of my doing
and the crooked angles of my hopes.
In them, I still say *no* to You
Who serenely asks for my *yes*.

Come, Lord Jesus, come and
hold me—hold my face
in Your hands until I see
Your face pull *yes, yes* from
a newly opened heart. Amen.

What All the Father Means in Me

Lord Jesus, when You walked
this earth as I now walk it,
You daily came to know
what all the Father meant for You.
You took then what came, and
*the tree, made sound, brought forth
good fruit*, Your heart always open
to what the Father might now ask
of You, His Son,
and You answered from Your heart
even when You told the Father
what the cost would be of
finishing the work You gave me to do.
Lord Jesus, watching Your courage
raising life from death, I set myself
to pull from my own heart
what all the Father means in me.
But this I know I have to beg:
no matter what the cost. Amen.

About the Author

Joseph A. Tetlow, SJ, was ordained in 1960. He has lectured, given retreats, and written extensively on Ignatian spirituality. With a doctorate in American social and intellectual history, he has been an editor of *America* magazine and formator for younger Jesuit priests. He was Assistant for Ignatian Spirituality to the Jesuit General in Rome, lecturing and giving retreats on all five continents. His *Choosing Christ in the World* (1987) was the earliest guide for making the Exercises in Daily Life and, now in several languages, continues in use. Of his more recent books, *Making Choices in Christ* explores the theology of the *Exercises; Finding Christ in the World* applies it through prayer to everyday life; and *Always Discerning* (named best book on spirituality by the Catholic Press Association) deals with the Ignatian experience of discernment. Fr. Tetlow continues to lecture and write. He resides at Montserrat Jesuit Retreat House in Lake Dallas, Texas.

More Books by Joseph A. Tetlow, SJ

PB | 978-0-8294-4456-8 | $14.95

Always Discerning
An Ignatian Spirituality for the New Millennium

Pope Francis has explicitly and repeatedly stated that discernment is essential for anyone who is a follower of Jesus Christ. But what, exactly, is discernment? Why must we do it? When do we do it? How should we do it?

In *Always Discerning*, Joseph A. Tetlow, SJ, delves thoughtfully into these questions and shares how lay Christians can implement discernment into not only life's big decisions but also into the everyday, more mundane choices we constantly find ourselves having to make. Guided by Scripture, Pope Francis's own words, and Ignatian spirituality, Fr. Tetlow helps us see that the dynamic interrelationship of head, heart, and hands is crucial to the discernment process.

To Order:

More Books by Joseph A. Tetlow, SJ

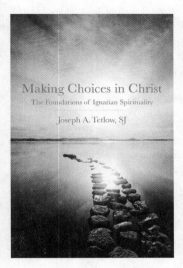

PB | 978-0-8294-2716-5 | $12.95

Making Choices in Christ
The Foundations of Ignatian Spirituality

In *Making Choices in Christ*, Joseph A. Tetlow, SJ, reveals how the ordinary person in modern times can embrace Ignatian spirituality through the extraordinary theology of St. Ignatius of Loyola and the Jesuits. This warmly written "field guide" to living Ignatian spirituality contains 40 concise meditations exploring what Ignatian spirituality is and isn't; what it means to live by it; Ignatius's legacy to all who practice Ignatian spirituality; and its important concepts and experiences, most notably the Spiritual Exercises.

Making Choices in Christ is an ideal resource to be used before or during a retreat with the Exercises, but it is also a great resource for the layperson who is curious about the "Jesuit mystique."

To Order:

Call 800.621.1008, visit store.loyolapress.com, or visit your local bookseller.

Related Books

PB | 978-0-8294-2120-0 | $12.95

Hearts on Fire
Praying with Jesuits

MICHAEL HARTER, SJ

Discover the rich tradition of Ignatian prayer in *Hearts on Fire*, compiled by Michael Harter, SJ. Hundreds of Ignatian prayers are included here, many written by the most illustrious Jesuits—Ignatius Loyola, Francis Xavier, Gerard Manley Hopkins, Anthony de Mello, Karl Rahner, Pierre Teilhard de Chardin, and others. Each gives eloquent voice to Ignatian spirituality, which affirms that God is present in all things and at all times. Thus, this collection includes Ignatian prayers for all occasions, including the most familiar and seemingly mundane.

To Order:

Call 800.621.1008, visit store.loyolapress.com, or visit your local bookseller.